Mamie Doud Eisenhower

Mamie Doud Eisenhower

★★★★★★★★★★★★★★★★★★★★★

1896–1979

BY SUSAN SINNOTT

CHILDREN'S PRESS®
A Division of Grolier Publishing
New York   London   Hong Kong   Sydney
Danbury, Connecticut

Consultant: LINDA CORNWELL
Coordinator of School Quality and Professional Improvement
Indiana State Teachers Association

Project Editor: DOWNING PUBLISHING SERVICES
Page Layout: CAROLE DESNOES
Photo Researcher: JAN IZZO

Visit Children's Press on the Internet at:
http://publishing.grolier.com

Library of Congress Cataloging-in-Publication Data
Sinnott, Susan.
     Mamie Doud Eisenhower, 1896–1979 / by Susan Sinnott
       p.   cm. — (Encyclopedia of first ladies)
     Includes bibliographical references and index.
     Summary: A biography of the wife of the thirty-fourth president of the United States, an
excellent White House hostess and a popular First Lady who did not involve herself in politics.
     ISBN 0-516-20599-4
     1. Eisenhower, Mamie Doud, 1896–1979—Juvenile literature. 2. Presidents' spouses—
United States—Biography—Juvenile literature. [1. Eisenhower, Mamie Doud, 1896–1979
2. First ladies. 3. Women—Biography] I. Title II. Title: Mamie Doud Eisenhower. III. Series
E837.S46   2000
973.921′092—dc 21   99–16785
[B]   CIP

Table of Contents

Mamie Doud Eisenhower

CHAPTER ONE

In the Pink

✶ ✶ ✶ ✶ ✶ ✶ ✶ ✶ ✶ ✶ ✶ ✶ ✶ ✶ ✶ ✶

The evening went by in a swirl of pink crinoline petticoats, shimmering silk, and black tuxedos. The new president, Dwight David Eisenhower—always called simply "Ike"—and his First Lady, Mamie, went to several inaugural balls. Every time they stepped out of their black limousine, the two thousand pink rhinestones hand sewn onto Mamie's gown glittered in the flashing lights of news cameras. "By golly, Mamie, you're beautiful!" Ike had said more than once as he looked over at his "girlfriend," as he called her after nearly forty years of marriage. Mamie's answering smile sparkled as brightly as any jewel.

✶ ✶ ✶ ✶ ✶ ✶ ✶ ✶ ✶ ✶ ✶ ✶ ✶ ✶ ✶ ✶

Mamie and Ike (right) chat with a group of people attending an inaugural ball.

The president was at his desk in the Oval Office by eight o'clock the morning after his inauguration.

Even after dancing until well past midnight, the new president was up and in the Oval Office by eight the next morning. (At 7:30, he was seen asking a White House usher where he might *find* his new office.) The staff was told, however, that Mrs. Eisenhower generally liked to sleep in. After the previous night's inaugural balls, they assumed half the day would probably go by before they heard from her. Yet, much to the surprise of head White House usher Howell Crim, the first call from Mrs. Eisenhower came before nine.

Mr. Crim and his assistant ran up the stairs to the White House family quarters and then waited in the sitting room outside the First Lady's bedroom. Finally, a maid came out of the bedroom and told them to walk right in. When they did, they "stopped dead in our tracks," as the ushers remembered. Mrs. Eisenhower was sitting up in bed surrounded by dozens of pink pillows. She wore a pink quilted-satin robe and a large pink bow in her hair. And she was smoking! The two ushers could scarcely believe their eyes. As they stood staring, Mamie Eisenhower

The Eisenhowers with chief usher Howell Crim (second from left) and his wife (right)

leaned over, flicked an ash from her cigarette onto her breakfast tray, and then flashed her dazzling smile.

"Every woman over fifty," Mamie once told a reporter, "should stay in bed until noon." Yet the entire White House staff soon realized that although the new First Lady would spend most of the morning in bed, she wouldn't be idle. Within a few weeks, she made the bedroom just the way she wanted it.

Out went the old double bed and in came a king-sized one with a pink satin pincushion headboard. She called her pink outpost "Mamie's command center" and, like a general's headquarters, she gave orders, planned the day's schedules and menus, worked on her correspondence, and spoke with members of the White House staff.

When she did get out of bed and dressed for the day, she attended

First Lady Mamie Eisenhower held her first press conference, intended mainly for women reporters, on March 12, 1953.

On her first day in the White House, January 21, 1953, Mamie held her first official tea, at which the honored guests were prominent Republican women.

Mamie's warmth and charm made her very popular along the campaign trail in 1952. She and Ike are shown here at a campaign event in St. Paul, Minnesota.

luncheons or teas for the many women's groups who came to the White House to visit the First Lady. Mamie, always happy at the center of attention, stood on a pedestal so that she could be seen by all the visitors. Women flocked to see her. She was one of them, they believed, devoted to husband, family, and the home—a true woman of the 1950s.

Mamie made no apologies for her likes and dislikes or for her old-fashioned folksy ways. All along the campaign trail in 1952, the press had tried to criticize Mamie for her girlish hairstyle, her love of pink, and her insistence on leaving all "important talk" to Ike. Yet her warmth and charm had made her a popular campaigner. In fact, calls of "We Like Mamie" rang

"I Like Ike"

✫ ✫ ✫ ✫ ✫ ✫ ✫ ✫ ✫ ✫ ✫ ✫ ✫ ✫ ✫ ✫ ✫ ✫ ✫ ✫

American presidential campaigns are typically boisterous, colorful contests. Along with bumper stickers, buttons, and banners, no campaign would be complete without a flurry of slogans. "Tippecanoe and Tyler, Too" chanted William Henry Harrison's supporters in 1840. Lincoln backers proclaimed "An Honest Vote for Honest Abe" in 1860. In 1964, Democrats for Lyndon Baines Johnson went "All the Way with LBJ." In the mid-1950s, however, Dwight Eisenhower's presidential campaigns popularized one of the most successful—and simple—political slo-

gans in American history. "I Like Ike" adorned everything from campaign buttons to ladies' stockings. Loyal Republican women wore "I Like Ike" rhinestone earrings; men sported ties bearing the slogan and a likeness of the candidate. The catchy phrase followed Ike through two successful presidential campaigns, in 1952 and 1956, and was much imitated and modified. "I Like Ike and Dick" included vice-presidential candidate Richard Nixon, and "I Like Mamie" voiced a vote of confidence for the aspiring First Lady. In French ("J'aime Ike"), Spanish ("Me Gusta Ike"), and Italian ("Mi Piace Ike"), voters expressed their multilingual support for the popular Dwight Eisenhower.

out at rallies just as often as the famous "We Like Ike!" Readers of women's magazines found her femininity and devotion to her wifely duties just what they liked in these years of postwar prosperity. She didn't apologize for her full-length mink coat, her love of delicate finery, or her trademark short bangs. Mamie wouldn't change and that was that. She was secure in the love of her husband and family and even a large part of the American public, so why should she worry about critics?

It hadn't always been like this. There had been long stretches when no one—not even Ike—seemed to care about her. During World War II, when General Eisenhower was the supreme commander of the Allied forces and lived in London, Mamie faded so far into the background it seemed she'd remain there forever. Ike was the man of the hour, the "army's pinup boy," as Mamie had once complained to a friend. Every time his photograph appeared in *Life* magazine or the *Saturday Evening Post*, his pretty English driver, Kay Summersby, was nearby. Whispers of a wartime ro-

During World War II, General Dwight Eisenhower was supreme commander of the Allied forces.

Kay Summersby, Ike's pretty English driver, attaching a flag to the general's car

During the Eisenhower Special whistle-stop campaign of 1952, Mamie Eisenhower often greeted the enthusiastic crowds dressed in her bathrobe.

mance between the two grew into open talk on both sides of the Atlantic. Mamie, in Washington, preferred to stay in her apartment rather than face the humiliating fact of "another woman."

Then, after loving words from a close family member, she did what she had done over and over during her long years as an army wife, she forced herself back to life. She dug deeply within and resolved to face each day with courage and determination—and she'd do it for the love of Ike.

During the 1952 presidential campaign, Mamie's face become almost as well known as that of her husband, the war hero. The Eisenhower Special, a nineteen-car train, took the Republican party nominee to nearly 80 whistle-stops in 45 states. Mamie loved greeting the enthusiastic crowds, sometimes even in her bathrobe and hair curlers. Whenever Ike visited a

Huge crowds of people, many with campaign signs, mobbed the car carrying Ike (center, with arms raised) and Mamie as they arrived in Chicago to attend the Republican National Convention in July 1952.

local hall to make a campaign speech, the crowd would first call out "Where's Mamie?" Ike would look around and then a high-pitched "Here I am" came from behind the curtain. And then the general's wife would walk around the closed curtain to resounding applause. Mamie Eisenhower would throw her head back and drink in the crowd's approval.

* * * * * * * * * * * * * * *

CHAPTER TWO

Denver Belle

★ ★ ★ ★ ★ ★ ★ ★ ★ ★ ★ ★ ★ ★ ★ ★ ★ ★ ★

Mamie loved to tell about her father, John Doud, and his great passion for newfangled technology. Only a few years into the twentieth century, he bought a shiny new car and began a tradition of family drives. Each Sunday morning, John Doud put on his long white duster and driving goggles and walked proudly out to his garage. He lifted the heavy door, got into his beloved Stanley Steamer, backed it down the driveway, and parked it at the end of his front walk. There he sat, waiting for his wife and four daughters to emerge from their stately brick home.

Every week, exactly the same thing occurred. After

★ ★ ★ ★ ★ ★ ★ ★ ★ ★ ★ ★ ★ ★ ★ ★ ★ ★ ★

Profile of America, 1896: Progress and Poverty

✻ ✻

When Mamie Doud was born in 1896, America was hurtling toward the twentieth century. Driven forward by industry, machinery, automation, and electricity, the nation barreled along on rails of steel—inventing, building, and expanding. With the admission of Utah that year, the United States had 45 states and a population nearing 70 million. The new industrial giant of the world, America made and consumed goods at record rates. An acre of wheat that once took more than sixty hours to produce by hand could now be harvested mechanically in just three hours. In 1896, Henry Ford made the first in a long line of automobiles bearing his name, and Charles Brady King was the first to drive a motorcar on the streets of Detroit. In a New York City music hall, audiences thrilled for the first time to "flickers," or moving pictures. At home, women enjoyed the convenience of newfangled appliances like vacuum cleaners and irons made possible by the magic of electricity that so wondrously illuminated city streets and buildings.

Four million Americans owned bicycles, and a craze for outdoor sports encouraged a more strenuous and healthy lifestyle. Women's fashions reflected their more active lives of playing croquet, golf, and badminton. Styles became generally looser and less fussy, but showing an ankle still raised eyebrows. At the first Olympiad held in 1,500 years, an American became the first Olympic champion when John Connolly placed first in the triple jump.

In the midst of progress and plenty, however, America in 1896 suffered through the second year of a major economic depression. Unemployment and homelessness soared. To support their families, women and children entered the workforce. Immigrants from Europe, arriving by the millions, crowded into the cities even as jobs grew scarcer. As the poor working class expanded, their pitiful wages and dismal living conditions contrasted dramatically with the profits and pleasures of the upper classes. Workers staged violent labor protests and groups such as the United Mine Workers and the National Congress of Parents and

Teachers arose to counter the ill effects of industry and poverty on the nation's workers and their children.

For African Americans, 1896 was especially bleak, for it was then that the U.S. Supreme Court made legal the concept of "separate but equal." The ruling permitted the segregation of blacks and whites in public places and marked a low point in the black struggle for equality that had begun at the end of the Civil War. Ironically, Harriet Beecher Stowe, whose book *Uncle Tom's Cabin* had moved so many Americans against slavery, died the same year. And in Washington, D.C., the house where President Abraham Lincoln died in 1865, shortly after freeing the slaves, became a national memorial.

two or three blasts of the horn, John Doud—called Pupah by his girls—finally got out of the car, bounded up the front steps, and stormed into the house. "Five minutes," he bellowed. "You are five minutes late!" Within seconds, Mrs. Doud, Eleanor, Mamie, Ida Mae, and Frances scurried onto the porch, pinning on their flowered hats and giggling.

One of them surely tweaked Pupah's cheek and soon his anger was gone completely. Before long, the family would be at one of their favorite spots, Cheesman Park. There, the girls would leap out of the car and run to the spot near the reflecting pool where a bronze marker pointed out all

The Doud family on a Sunday outing in the car that was John Doud's proudest possession

the high peaks of the Colorado Rockies, just west of Denver.

John Doud had always been a restless man. Born in Chicago, his father moved to Boone, Iowa, where he started a successful meatpacking business. John attended Northwestern University and the University of Chicago, but traveled around the country—even working for a while on a Mississippi riverboat—before returning to Boone to learn the family business. Shortly after he arrived home, he met a beautiful Swedish girl named Elivera Carlson. Elivera was only six-

John Doud poses in the driver's seat of his car as his wife sits in the back. The four Doud girls are on the porch with two members of the household staff.

Mamie's maternal grandfather, Carl Carlson, owned this mill in Boone, Iowa.

Happily Horseless

✫ ✫

The Doud family motorcar outings reflected a new passion sweeping the country: automobiling. The first successful automobiles had been introduced in the United States in the 1890s, and Americans were hooked. Early models included gasoline, electric, and steam-powered varieties like the Stanley Steamer developed by twin brother inventors Francis and Freelan Stanley. These cars ran on steam from a fire-heated boiler. Their popularity faded after oil was discovered in Texas in 1901 and gasoline became cheap and plentiful. The first commercially successful car was called an Oldsmobile, built by Ransom Olds that same year. No matter what cars they drove, however, the first motorists faced the same chal-

An 1899 Stanley Steamer

lenges. Early autos clattered and sputtered, spewing smoke and smell. They terrified horses and pedestrians—and often passengers. A confusing jumble of newly written traffic laws attempted to slow cars down to a horse's pace. Vermonters even adopted an English law requiring an adult carrying a red flag to walk in front of every car. Paved roads were few, so motorists tackled dusty, muddy, rutted roads and emerged covered with dirt from their open cars. Stylish new motoring fashions included long coats called dusters to protect clothing; goggles for the eyes; and for ladies, large-brimmed hats secured with yards of veiling. With breakdowns common, "automobilists" were advised to carry tools, spare parts, and an emergency food kit, including two pounds of sweet chocolate.

teen, but John Doud wasn't interested in waiting for his bride to grow up. He proposed within months of their first introduction, and Elivera and John were married in 1894.

The Douds' first daughter, Eleanor, was born in 1895 and the next year another girl, Mamie Geneva, arrived. Two more girls, Mabel Frances and Ida Mae, arrived after John's expanding business caused him to move the family to Cedar Rapids. Even though Cedar Rapids was just about 100 miles

Mamie Geneva Doud (left) at the age of one with her sister Eleanor, who was two

24

(161 kilometers) east of Boone, Elivera Doud missed her close-knit Swedish family terribly. She insisted that she and her four young daughters take the train to Boone nearly every weekend. On the coldest days of January, Grandpa Carlson met the Doud girls at the train station with a horse-drawn sleigh. Mamie and her sisters, covered with a thick buffalo robe, were wedged closely together in the back seat. They warmed their feet on hot bricks.

These visits highlighted the deep differences between fun-loving John Doud and his more practical and serious wife Elivera. Nothing gave John more pleasure than spoiling his daughters. Yet Elivera, whose family was prosperous but strictly religious, believed pure indulgence was a sin. She scolded him for his generous gifts and

25

indulgent ways, but he ignored her pleas to change.

As Mamie grew into adolescence, she clearly became her father's girl. She came to dread the visits to Boone, where her exuberant high spirts had to be stifled. She couldn't play cards or games in Boone. "All we could do was sit on the steps and watch people go by," Mamie recalled many years later.

John Doud loved pranks and, sensing that Mamie was a kindred spirit,

John and Elivera Doud with their daughters (left to right) Ida Mae, Mabel Frances, Eleanor, and Mamie

The Douds' home in Cedar Rapids

always included her in his fun. The Douds were the first family in Cedar Rapids to have a telephone and John Doud put it to use staging phone calls from Santa Claus or the birthday angel. One of these calls told Mamie where she might find her special birthday present that year: a small diamond ring in a gold filigree setting.

Just as Mamie was beginning school, John Doud decided to sell his business in Cedar Rapids and move his family west to Colorado Springs, Colorado. He hoped the thin mountain air would strengthen Eleanor's fragile health. But it did almost the opposite. In Colorado Springs, Eleanor developed a rheumatic heart condition and needed full-time nursing care. John Doud, frantic to try something else, moved the family to Denver.

At the start of the twentieth century, Denver was a boomtown. Many families had become wealthy through mining and the cattle business. John Doud, whose business ventures had earned him more than a million dollars, moved into Denver society with ease. He bought a large brick house in

Mamie Doud was born in this house at 709 Carroll Street in Boone, Iowa.

Downtown Denver as it looked about 1900, near the time the Douds moved to Colorado

one of the nicest parts of the city. With several servants to perform household tasks, the family was free to live a life of ease. They went to band concerts and picnics in city parks and went into the mountains to ride horses and to fish. And, of course, there were Daddy's Sunday drives.

When the Douds came home on Sunday evenings, they held an open house. A buffet table was set and anyone who wanted could come in for food, conversation, and poker. Mamie's mother and sisters loved to decorate their buffet table for every holiday—hearts on Valentine's Day, pumpkins and ghosts for Halloween— long before most people bothered with such things. Birthdays meant that one became queen for the day, with a special procession down the front steps to loud singing of "Here Comes the Bride." "It was a girl family," Mamie once explained.

In 1910, because of Eleanor's continued poor health, John Doud de-

John Doud bought this large house in one of the nicest parts of Denver.

Mamie (second from right) with friends enjoying a picnic in a Denver city park

cided that the family should begin spending the long winters farther south. He rented a large house in San Antonio, Texas, pulled his daughters out of school, and, late in October, loaded his household into two touring cars and set off.

Despite John and Elivera Douds' devotion, Eleanor's heart condition did not improve. She died of heart failure in 1912, at the age of seventeen. The family was devastated by her death. John Doud, who always thought there was something more he could do to keep death away, took Eleanor's loss as a personal blow.

Mamie later remembered that, suddenly, her parents seemed as devoted to Eleanor's death as they had been to her life. Every day for three months, they took a streetcar to the Denver cemetery where she was buried. Eventually, they settled into a routine of going once a week to take fresh flowers. These visits, as regular as the Sunday drives and open houses once had been, made a strong impression on Mamie. She long remembered the family standing at the tombstone and the low, sad sound of the birds in the

Mamie (second from left) with her Central Presbyterian Church Sunday School class, Easter 1913

In the fall of 1914, when she was eighteen years old, Mamie was enrolled at Miss Wolcott's School.

nearby cypress trees. She had loved her older sister, but this long mourning period made life seem much too grim. Mamie wanted fun and laughter to return to their lives.

The Douds' lifestyle of travel and change, punctuated by the upheaval of Eleanor's illness and death, meant that none of the girls had gone to school for more than a few years at a time. Mamie attended school while she was either in Denver or in San Antonio, but in between she simply didn't go. Her father didn't believe good grades or study habits were important for girls. Along with most men of his day, he thought girls would get quite enough of the necessary training at home, watching their mothers oversee servants and learning to entertain the right kind of society.

In the fall of 1914, however, when Mamie was eighteen, John Doud decided Mamie should attend school a bit more regularly. She was enrolled at Denver's exclusive Miss Wolcott's, which had been founded as a school for "ladies of refinement." But Mamie found her studies quite dull compared with the larger world of parties and

The fall of 1915 was Mamie Doud's debutante season, when she was formally presented to society.

dances that awaited her. The fall of 1915 was Mamie's debutante season, and her fun-loving charm had made her one of the most popular young ladies in Denver.

That October, when the rest of her family prepared to return to San Antonio, Mamie begged Pupah to let her quit school and come with them. John

During her debutante year, Mamie had many formal studio photographs taken.

Mamie Doud's fun-loving charm made her one of the most popular young ladies in Denver.

Doud couldn't resist her pleas, and so Mamie said a happy farewell to Miss Wolcott's. She said goodbye, too, to the young men who gathered around her front porch, hoping to take her out for dinner and dancing. As John Doud's shiniest, newest car backed out of their driveway at the end of 1915, Mamie blew kisses and waved her hankie goodbye. "Don't worry," she called out, "I'll be back again in June."

CHAPTER THREE

You're in the Army Now . . .

☆ ☆ ☆ ☆ ☆ ☆ ☆ ☆ ☆ ☆ ☆ ☆ ☆ ☆ ☆

For many of Denver's society girls, life's path was all but certain. After a "coming-out" year of balls, parties, and many suitors, some young man from another upper-class family would soon ask for the debutante's hand in marriage. After an elegant society wedding, the young couple would begin their own life of luxury and comfort.

The course of Mamie Doud's life, however, took a sharp turn in San Antonio that winter of 1915–1916. One Sunday afternoon, John Doud suggested including some family friends, the Harrises, on their weekly drive. Since Mrs. Harris's sister was married to an army

☆ ☆ ☆ ☆ ☆ ☆ ☆ ☆ ☆ ☆ ☆ ☆ ☆ ☆ ☆

Those Dazzling Debutantes

✫ ✫

The word *debutante* comes from a French word meaning "to begin." A debutante is a young woman in her late teens who is being officially introduced, or "presented," to society as a way of announcing her eligibility for marriage. A debutante is often said to be "coming out." Though considered old-fashioned today, the debutante tradition was once an important ritual among America's well-to-do families. The custom has its roots in eighteenth-century England, where the aristocracy felt it important to marry their daughters to husbands who made a suitable financial and social match. At marriageable age, these daughters were "presented" during a social round of parties and fanfare so that young men might know of their availability. The luckiest young ladies were presented to the royal family in London at the start of the social season in April. A swirl of festivities and parties lasted through July, leading, hopefully, to a series of engagements. In colonial America, "dancing assemblies" were the forerunner of the twentieth-century debutante balls, which are still held during the social season between November and January. Traditionally, during her debutante year, a young woman gave and attended parties, surrounded herself with a "court" of attendants, and received much attention in the newspapers' society pages. She concluded her year with a lavish ball attended by family, friends, suitors, and other debs. There, elegantly turned out in a white evening gown, she made her official bow to society as a marriageable young sophisticate. Though the tradition continues in many elite circles today, the emphasis has shifted from finding an appropriate mate to entering the adult world of social, civic, and cultural responsibility.

officer and currently living at San Antonio's Fort Sam Houston, someone suggested going there for a visit. Once there, the Douds and the Harrises sat on the front porch sipping lemonade. Across the way, a young officer walked out of another house, waved, and then came over to meet the Harrises'

San Antonio's Fort Sam Houston Infantry Post entrance about 1910

In 1915, Dwight D. Eisenhower was a senior at the United States Military Academy at West Point, New York

friends. He introduced himself as Lieutenant Dwight Eisenhower and then chatted politely before excusing himself to make his rounds. Just before leaving, however, he turned to Mamie and asked if she'd like to join him. Mamie quickly accepted and hopped down from the porch.

The young officer was immediately struck by Miss Doud's spunk and sassiness. When he matter-of-factly told her that, since this was an army base and the men weren't expecting ladies, she should keep her eyes straight ahead, Mamie immediately turned her head from side to side. When she flashed Lieutenant Eisenhower an impish smile, he was completely smitten.

As their love grew during that winter, neither paid much attention to the differences in their backgrounds. Opposites attract, Mamie liked to say, and the Douds and the Eisenhowers were certainly that. If the Douds were a "girl family"—devoted to parties and frills—the Eisenhowers were a rough-and-tumble "boy family." While the Douds were wealthy and the girls

Mamie Doud about 1916, not long after she met Dwight Eisenhower in San Antonio, Texas

The Eisenhower family at the time Ike (left) was ten years old. His brothers Edgar, Earl, Arthur, and Roy are in the back row (left to right). Milton is in the front between his parents, David and Ida.

This series of pictures shows Dwight David Eisenhower as a three-year-old, at the age of ten, and as a cadet at the United States Military Academy at West Point.

pampered and spoiled, the Eisenhowers—from Abilene, Kansas—had struggled to feed their five sons during a deep economic depression. They'd needed to rely on the hard work of every family member. While John and Elivera Doud kept up appearances for their own sake, Ike's mother and father valued Christian duty and service above all else.

After that first afternoon together, Ike couldn't get Mamie out of his mind. Her breezy, devil-may-care spirit intrigued him, and he called for her several times a day although he al-most never found her home. ("What did he expect?" Mamie later remembered. "I was booked solid. It was my debutante year!") Yet not only was he not put off by her unavailability, he found it part of her attractiveness. While Mamie was out on a date with another young man, Dwight would come to her house and sit on the veranda with Mr. and Mrs. Doud. Finally, her father mentioned to Mamie that if she didn't stop "that flighty nonsense" the "army boy" would forget about her altogether.

Mamie finally agreed to have din-

A 1910 picture of David and Ida Eisenhower (seated) with their sons (left to right) Milton, Dwight, and Earl

The Abilene, Kansas, home of the Eisenhowers about 1895. Posing in front are (left to right) Dwight, Edgar, Earl, Roy, and Arthur.

ner with Dwight at a nearby restaurant. Then they went dancing. Shortly after that, Mamie stopped seeing other boys altogether. By the end of 1915, her father wrote to her with some regret that he knew she would soon leave "to be someone's little woman." That Christmas, Ike gave Mamie a silver box with her initials engraved on it. Mamie said the present was so "intimate" that she had to ask her father if she could keep it.

In March, when Ike asked for Mamie's hand, John Doud asked only that the couple hold off the marriage until after Mamie's twentieth birthday on November 14. When a late-fall wedding date was agreed to, Ike surprised Mamie with a large diamond engagement ring. Everyone wondered how a young army officer had managed the cost with his meager army earnings. Mamie worried that he'd be in debt for years to come. The truth, however, was that his earnings from a few lucky poker games quickly paid for the ring.

Despite John Doud's careful planning, Mamie was destined to be a teenage bride. Not for the last time would her life with Ike be twisted and turned by international conflict. This time, it was tension along the nearby United States border with Mexico. The famous Mexican rebel Pancho Villa was attacking towns along the Rio Grande, and army officers at San Antonio's Fort Sam Houston were on alert. Army leaves were canceled and only fast talking by young Lieutenant Eisenhower made it possible for Ike and Mamie to wed at all that year. When Ike did secure a leave late in June, he wired Mamie in Denver that he was on his way to marry her. The Douds were "speechless" and worried that any ceremony held so quickly would raise eyebrows. But Mamie, as usual, didn't care about their objections. John and Elivera Doud realized it was useless to stand in her way.

At noon on July 1, 1916, Mamie Geneva Doud descended the staircase of her parents' Denver home and took the arm of her handsome army officer, who had just been promoted to first lieutenant. She wore white lace, which in her hurry she'd had to buy "off the rack" at a Denver store. Ike was in his dress-white uniform, with

Francisco "Pancho" Villa (1878–1923)

✫ ✫ ✫ ✫ ✫ ✫ ✫ ✫ ✫ ✫ ✫ ✫ ✫ ✫ ✫ ✫ ✫ ✫ ✫ ✫

Born Doroteo Arango to a peasant family, this famous revolutionary grew up in a Mexico sharply divided between rich hacienda owners and the impoverished laborers who worked their lands. Young Doroteo tried to escape the hard life of his parents. To avenge an attack on his sister, he murdered a landowner's son and fled to the mountains. He took the name Francisco (Pancho for short) Villa and lived

as a bandit. When Mexico plunged into revolution in 1910, Villa rallied to the cause of the lower classes. His intimate knowledge of the land and his huge following made him an important ally. His command skills, quick temper, and ready use of force made him a frightening enemy. He took control of northern Mexico, and by 1913 had gained international fame. So successful was he in defeating government troops that the world believed Pancho Villa would be the next president of Mexico. After Villa endured a series of bloody losses, however, the United States withdrew its support. Villa retaliated with attacks on Americans that culminated in the New Mexico town of Columbus, which he and his "Villistas" raided and burned in 1916. For a year after the attack, American troops searched the Mexican mountains unsuccessfully for Pancho Villa. When the Mexican government collapsed in 1920, Villa, age forty-three, ended his revolutionary work. The new president granted him a pardon and gave him a ranch where he lived peacefully, striving to ensure a decent life and education for his employees. Despite these final quiet years, Pancho Villa died as violently as he had lived, by assassins' bullets in 1923.

creases so starched that he didn't dare sit down until after the ceremony. They exchanged vows before a minister in front of the fireplace and then went into the dining room for a formal luncheon. After a few days at a mountain resort near Denver, Mr. and Mrs. Dwight D. Eisenhower boarded a train for Abilene, Kansas, where Mamie would meet Ike's parents for the first time.

Mamie bit her lip more than a few times during that first trip to the Eisenhower home. Even though they were in Abilene only a short time, she noticed so many things about Ike's upbringing that were different from her own. Ike's father, David, for example, met the train in his shirtsleeves. Why, John Doud would never have left his home without a jacket even in the heat of the summer! And when Ike's mother hosted a family brunch that day, Mamie was amazed that she and her sons did all the cooking and cleaning themselves. There wasn't a servant in sight! By the time they got on the train later that day for San Antonio, Mamie had seen a completely different side of the Eisenhowers. She only

The newlyweds at St. Louis College, where Ike coaches the football team in his spare time

Ike's parents, David and Ida Eisenhower in their Abilene home

In 1898, the Eisenhowers moved into this larger house in Abilene.

ment into a home. There was only one problem. Since she'd always had servants and cooks in her home, Mamie had few homemaking skills. Ike soon realized that if he wanted to eat a decent meal in his own kitchen, he would have to cook it himself.

Mamie had also been warned about the rigid formality of army life. She had been told that her husband would be away often and that she would be expected to carry on without complaining. At nineteen, she'd nodded yes to all this without really knowing what it would be like. When she began to find out within the first weeks of their marriage, she protested loudly. She and Ike began to quarrel

hoped the old saying "opposites attract" did hold true after all.

In San Antonio, Mamie set herself to turning their two-room army apart-

and he openly wondered if Mamie would ever lose her pampered debutante ways. A month after the wedding, when Ike announced that his job would take him away for a while, Mamie cried and pleaded with him not to go. When she questioned how he could possibly stand to be away from her, he pulled her close to him and said, lovingly but firmly, "My duty will always come first." That night, and many nights afterward, Mamie cried herself to sleep.

Newlyweds Ike and Mamie Eisenhower in 1916 at Fort Sam Houston, Texas

The newlywed Eisenhowers lived in a two-room apartment at Fort Sam Houston (lower left in this picture).

CHAPTER FOUR

"A Grief . . . that Would Break the Hardest Heart"

★ ★ ★ ★ ★ ★ ★ ★ ★ ★ ★ ★ ★ ★ ★ ★ ★ ★

The year after Mamie and Ike were married—1917—saw America's entrance into World War I. From the safety of Fort Sam Houston, the young couple watched the events in Europe with eager interest. Mamie fretted that her new husband was about to be lost to the faraway battlefront. Ike worried that he *wouldn't* be sent to Europe and would instead spend the war on the sidelines.

Lieutenant Eisenhower's fears were realized when he learned that half of his regiment was to be sent to France but that he was to go to Camp Oglethorpe,

★ ★ ★ ★ ★ ★ ★ ★ ★ ★ ★ ★ ★ ★ ★ ★ ★ ★

World War I: Fast Facts

WHAT: The "Great War," the "War to End All Wars," the first truly global conflict

WHEN: 1914–1918

WHO: The Central European Powers, including Austria-Hungary and Germany, opposed the Allied Powers, including Britain, France, and Russia. The United States entered the war on the Allied side in 1917.

WHERE: The Central Powers invaded Serbia, Romania, Russia, Belgium, France, and Italy. Fighting extended into the Atlantic Ocean and the Mediterranean Sea.

WHY: European disputes over land, economics, religion, and leadership boiled over in 1914 when Austrian archduke Francis Ferdinand was assassinated on a visit to Serbia. Austria declared war on Serbia, and other European nations joined in. The United States got involved largely because German submarine warfare disrupted commerce in the North Atlantic Ocean.

OUTCOME: The Central Powers fell to the Allied Powers in 1918, and an armistice was signed on November 11. The map of Europe was redrawn and the League of Nations was founded to settle international disputes. Ten million soldiers, including 116,500 Americans, had died.

Lieutenant Dwight Eisenhower (left) training soldiers for trench warfare

Doud Dwight (Icky) Eisenhower was born on September 24, 1917.

Georgia, to train officers in trench warfare. He was bitterly disappointed, and Mamie tried to console him as best she could. Since she'd also just learned that she was expecting their first child in the fall of 1917, she allowed herself to mix relief with sympathy.

Mamie spent the long, hot Texas summer alone at the army base. Her mother joined her at the end of August and was with her on September 24 when Mamie went into labor. The two women caught a ride on a mule-drawn wagon that shuttled army men around Fort Sam Houston. In a dark room in the base infirmary, Mamie gave birth to a healthy boy, Doud

47

Life in the Trenches

☆ ☆

Little in our experience today can compare with the horrors of trench warfare. And yet thousands of Allied and German soldiers spent World War I in the dirt and stink and terror of a maze of ditches that ran the length of the Western Front. From the North Sea, through France, to the Swiss border, the armies dug hundreds of miles of trenches. Between the Germans on one side and the Allies on the other stretched a desolate, scorched swath of earth called No Man's Land. The trenches were about 7 feet (2 meters) deep and 6 feet (1.8 m) wide, generally arranged in three rows. Men in the frontline trenches watched and waited nervously for enemy attack or for the frightening order to "go over the top"—to charge out of the trench into the open. Soldiers shared the trenches with rats and lice, and at the worst times stood knee-deep in water and mud. Men kept their heads low for fear of sniper fire, but the most terrifying attacks came in the form of poisonous gases that blinded, suffocated, and killed. Regular shell bombardments tore up the landscape. At night, patrols crept out of the trenches to mend barbed wire and to spy on the enemy. Despite the horror and ferocity of trench warfare, however, most of it amounted to little more than a standoff. For much of the war, neither side gained nor lost much more than 10 miles (16 kilometers) of ground along the length of the Western Front.

Dwight, who was promptly nicknamed Icky.

Mamie loved being a new mother but longed for the war to end and for Ike to be able to join her. Ike was an exuberant father but, ever the loyal army officer, he still hoped for the call to battle. The family stayed together briefly at a makeshift camp in Gettysburg and spent the following summer in a Gettysburg College fraternity house. When the cold months returned, the entire camp disassembled and prepared to move on.

This picture of Mamie, Ike, and Icky was probably taken in 1918.

Ike and Mamie spent the summer of 1918 in this Gettysburg College fraternity house.

Ike was so sure that he would be sent to Europe at this time that Mamie and the baby prepared to move to the Douds' home in Denver.

Mamie was very gloomy as she and Icky boarded a train in Harrisburg, Pennsylvania, and headed west. As they pulled into small towns—first in Ohio, then in Indiana—Mamie heard church bells. Then, when they arrived at Chicago's Union Station, there were so many people dancing and celebrating that Mamie could barely get through the crowd to make her connection for Denver.

When Mamie learned the reason for the celebration, a smile spread across her face for the first time in

When Mamie and Icky arrived at Chicago's Union Station on their way to Colorado, Mamie learned that World War I was over.

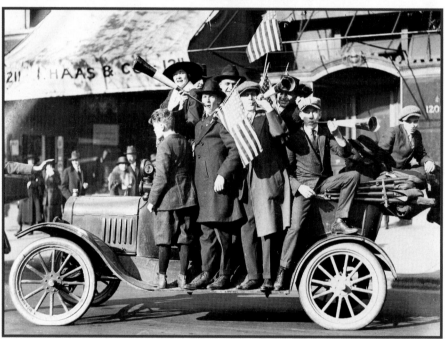

A Washington, D.C., Armistice Day celebration on November 11, 1918

weeks. The war was over! Ike would be able to come home after all.

In the fall of 1919, the Eisenhowers moved to Fort Meade, near Baltimore, Maryland. For the first time, they were able to live as a normal family. Two-year-old Icky was a bright, eager child and both parents were devoted to him. Ike worked long hours but came home every night. Mamie loved to entertain and held many parties at their home. At the end of most evenings, Mamie sat at the piano and played favorite songs so that everyone could sing along. Ike coached a Tank Corps football team and Icky was the team mascot, complete with his own uniform.

These were among the happiest times the Eisenhowers had known since they were married. Mamie knew it wouldn't last, that another transfer would send them to some remote base, but she vowed to enjoy every second at Fort Meade. On Christmas Eve 1920, she left Icky with her mother at Fort Meade and went into

Mamie, Ike, and Icky posed for this family picture in 1919.

Ike with the Tank Corps at Fort Meade, Maryland

51

When doctors at Fort Meade weren't sure what Icky's illness was, they consulted specialists at Johns Hopkins hospital (right).

nearby Baltimore with friends to shop. When she came home, her mother told her Icky wasn't well. After Mamie ran to his room and found him restless and feverish, she rushed him to the hospital. She passed the Christmas tree on the way out the door, and when Icky spotted a shiny red tricycle, he pointed. But he never came home. At first, the base doctors didn't think his illness was serious, but when Icky grew sicker, they consulted specialists at nearby Johns Hopkins Hospital and learned he had scarlet fever. "Within a week he was gone . . ." Mamie told her grand-

daughter Susan more than fifty years later. Icky died in his father's arms on January 2, 1921. Theirs was a grief, Ike later recalled, that "would have broken the hardest heart."

After Icky's death, the task of rejoining the world seemed almost unbearably sad. Mamie and Ike, each struggling with their own feelings, found it hard to face each other. Ike immersed himself in work, though he found it had less meaning for him. Mamie, who as a girl had hated her family's weekly visits to her older sister's grave in Denver, believed she needed to push death's sadness away.

*The Eisenhowers'
second son, John
Sheldon Doud, was
born on August 3,
1922.*

Grieving could be avoided, she told herself, if she only tried hard enough.

When the couple discovered less than a year later that Mamie was expecting another baby, the news was greeted with a mixture of joy and sadness. They hoped the new baby would relieve their sorrow. When John was born on August 3, 1922, Mamie threw herself back into motherhood, although she was overanxious about John's health and safety. She had trouble letting him out of her sight and fretted over every cough and sneeze. Family friends watched, first with amusement and then alarm, as Mamie

53

In the Zone

★ ★

The country of Panama in Central America occupies a narrow stretch of land between the Atlantic and Pacific Oceans. Before 1914, there was no way for ships sailing between New York and San Francisco to cross Panama's 50-mile (80-km) width. Instead, they sailed all the way around the tip of South America, making the voyage between the two cities an exhausting 13,000 miles (20,921 km). In 1903, the United States made a deal with Panama to build and operate a waterway, or canal, across its narrowest width. The canal would shorten the journey from the Atlantic to the Pacific by 7,800 miles (12,553 km)! It took thousands of laborers ten years and millions of dollars to claw through the earth and open a passage between the oceans. In 1914, the first ship passed through the canal. To maintain and administer the canal, the United States negotiated with Panama to govern a zone around it of about 650 square miles (1,684 sq km). At its peak, 36,000 Americans, called Zonians, lived in the Canal Zone. Many of them, like the Eisenhowers, were in the military. Panamanians wanted the land back, however, and the United States agreed to transfer the Zone back to Panama in 1979. At the end of 1999, Panama also took over the operation of the canal itself.

chased after John with hat and mittens long after he was old enough to take care of himself.

At the same time Mamie fretted over her second son, Ike was more distant than he had been with Icky. It seemed almost that the pain of losing Icky was so great that he was afraid to open himself to anyone again. Instead,

he became a stern disciplinarian, perhaps sometimes confusing his son with his new army recruits. Shortly after the Eisenhowers returned to Fort Meade from Icky's funeral, Ike was posted to Panama, a tropical outpost more than 2,000 miles (3,219 km) away. Ike, who believed this was a chance to move his career along, ac-

Mamie Eisenhower in Panama, where she and Ike lived from 1921 to 1924

cepted willingly. He privately hoped that leaving Fort Meade would make life a bit less sad.

Mamie wondered how she would bear living in the tropics. Her worst fears were realized when she arrived and saw that the family's living quarters were in a jungle clearing that could be reached only by a narrow footpath. Their house was a small wooden structure full of insects and bats, and it smelled of mildew from the heat and humidity.

Mamie hated life in the Canal Zone, but when she looked to Ike for understanding, he seemed lost to her. She made friends with the wife of another officer, who noticed Mamie's unhappiness. She saw that the couple had grown apart and suspected that they hadn't given each other a chance to heal from their son's death. This friend pointed out to Mamie that she would lose Ike if she didn't pull herself together. "You still haven't left your pampered girlhood behind," she suggested, "and you must if you are to be Ike's wife and helpmate." Mamie vowed—not for the last time—to pull herself together for Ike.

These pictures show Mamie Geneva Doud Eisenhower as she looked through the years. Above left: Mamie in 1923, at the time she and Ike were living in Panama; in 1925 (below left); in 1928 (above right); and in 1935 (below right).

Student Soldiers

★ ★

Steeped in a colorful history and governed by strict tradition, the United States Military Academy at West Point is the country's oldest service academy. Located high above New York's Hudson River, it began life during the Revolutionary War (1775–1783) as a fort built to defend the river from British warships. For added security, American troops blockaded the river with a giant iron chain stretching from bank to bank. In 1780, Benedict Arnold, West Point's treasonous commander, hatched a plot to deliver the fort to the British. After the plan failed, West Point was never again threatened. Today, it is the nation's oldest occupied military post. In 1802, Congress established the military academy there, and ten cadets began their training. West Point graduates fought on both sides during the Civil War, including Union general Ulysses S. Grant and Confederate leader Robert E. Lee. Over the years, the academy sharpened other famous military minds, including Generals MacArthur, Patton, Eisenhower, and Schwartzkopf. Today, the Corps of Cadets includes more than 4,000 men and women who study mathematics and engineering and receive intensive military training. Like Dwight Eisenhower in 1915 and his son John in 1944, successful West Point cadets receive the rank of second lieutenant in the army upon graduation.

West Point cadet John Eisenhower

The Eisenhowers' son John at the age of thirteen

Ike, Mamie, and John in the Philippines, 1937

By the time the Eisenhower family left Panama in 1924, their marriage was strong again. Mamie had begun to learn the hard job of taking the world as it is, not as she would have it. The demands of army life didn't let up. There were always new assignments, from Panama to Washington and then the Philippines. Both parents watched proudly as John moved through elementary school, high school, and then was accepted at West Point just as his father had been.

When John went off to college, Mamie and Ike found themselves once again at Fort Sam Houston, where their married life had begun. As they celebrated their twentieth wedding anniversary, Ike had surprised Mamie with the news of his promotion to lieutenant colonel. Back in San Antonio at the time of their twenty-fifth anniversary, Ike was made a full colonel.

By 1941, Dwight D. Eisenhower was a general and Europe was at war. On the Sunday afternoon of December 7, Mamie and Ike were at their Fort Sam Houston home. Suddenly, the radio blared the announcement

that the Japanese had bombed the U.S. naval base in Pearl Harbor, Hawaii. Ike immediately scrambled for his shoes. Mamie covered her face with her hands and wondered helplessly what would happen next.

After a few minutes, the phone rang. Ike picked it up and slammed it down again. He bolted for the door, concern etched in his face. As Mamie watched the door close behind the new general, she knew life would never be the same for them again.

This picture of Mamie at the Manila Hotel was Ike's favorite.

The Japanese attack on the U.S. naval base at Pearl Harbor, Hawaii (below), brought the United States into World War II.

CHAPTER FIVE

War Widow

There was no reason for Ike to worry that he'd miss this world war as he'd missed the last one. Within a few months of President Roosevelt's declaration of war, General Eisenhower received word of his assignment. Ike was surprised—"mildly startled," as his son John remembered—to learn he'd been appointed commanding general of U.S. Army forces in Europe. It was a breathtaking promotion and a sign that his superiors placed great confidence in him. It was also, Ike knew, a heavy responsibility.

The mood was quiet and serious when Ike left Washington for Allied headquarters in London. Mamie

World War II: Fast Facts

WHAT: The second great global conflict

WHEN: 1939–1945

WHO: The Axis powers, including Germany, Italy, and Japan, opposed the Allies, including Britain, France, and the USSR. The United States entered the war on the Allied side in 1941 after the bombing by Japan of Pearl Harbor in Hawaii.

WHERE: Fighting raged throughout the Pacific Ocean and in the Atlantic, as well as from Scandinavia to North Africa and deep into the Soviet Union.

WHY: Chancellor Adolf Hitler set out to make Germany the most powerful country in the world, and began by invading his European neighbors. Japan, Italy, and Germany pledged support to one another in 1940. When the United States declared war on Japan after the attack on Pearl Harbor in 1941, Germany and Italy declared war on the United States.

OUTCOME: The war ended in stages. Germany surrendered in May 1945. Japan surrendered after the United States dropped two atomic bombs there in August. More than 400,000 American troops died in battle; about 17 million on both sides perished.

Lieutenant General Dwight David Eisenhower, commanding general of U.S. Army forces in Europe

walked with him to the car that waited to take him to Bolling Air Force Base for the long flight across the North Atlantic. As the car pulled away, Ike reached out, grabbed Mamie's hand, and kissed it. He told her he'd asked the pilot to circle past the army base so that he could see her one more time. At the appointed time, Mamie ran across the lawn to the flagpole. When she spotted the plane, she jumped and waved her hands, and then she and

During Christmas 1943, Mamie Eisenhower posed for pictures at her piano. While Ike was in Europe, she was living in a one-bedroom apartment at the Wardman Towers complex in Washington, D.C.

two friends yelled "Happy Landings" at the top of their lungs.

Within a week, Mamie moved out of her home at the army base to a one-bedroom apartment at the Wardman Towers complex. Many other army wives planned to wait out the war there as well, and, before long, a group of them began to meet for drinks, potluck dinners, cards, and "girl talk," as Mamie called it.

As much as Mamie enjoyed these social gatherings, she found it more and more difficult to keep up other activities. Succumbing to war widow's depression, she cut back most of her activities and seemed to live only for Ike's letters, which usually came three times a week. "I cannot tell you how much I miss you," he wrote in the first, dated June 26, 1942. ". . . I constantly find myself wondering 'why isn't

Mamie here?' " What little energy Mamie had was eaten up by worry over Ike's safety and keeping a scrapbook of clippings about him.

Mamie's family and friends worried about Mamie's increasing isolation and depression and encouraged her to socialize. She refused to go to the movies since she would see newsreels of London and the bombings. Most likely, too, she'd see Ike on the screen, surveying the damage or planning the next counterattack. He would look so strong and certain. Mamie fretted

Mamie pinned a medal on Ike, the new supreme commander of the Allied Invasion Forces, as President Manuel Quezon of the Philippines looked on.

General Eisenhower holding a news conference at his London headquarters in 1942

that, in contrast, she was too weak and nervous. "My husband has become a pinup boy," she told a friend uncertainly.

Increasingly, these pictures and newsreels featured a dark, pretty woman standing near Ike. This was Kay Summersby, an Irish-born member of the Royal Women's Auxiliary Corps. Kay, a former model and actress, was General Eisenhower's official driver. As rumors about a wartime romance swirled about, Mamie's morale weakened further.

Mamie spent nearly every evening with the other officers' wives, who were as lonely, bored, and anxious about the war as she was. Drinks were always served before dinner and

Mamie avoided going to the movies so that she wouldn't see newsreels showing the bombings over Europe.

General Eisenhower (center) conferring with other officers at the War Plans Division Headquarters in London

Mamie found that two, then three drinks, made her fears go away. She could have a moment of peace, which she badly needed. Yet those watching her knew the price of Mamie's peace would be high. Ike would be livid to know that she found comfort from whiskey. He would feel let down and possibly never forgive her. And the press surely would find out sooner or later. In fact, reporters had already begun peering into Mamie's life, looking for the human-interest stories their readers wanted. A family friend who was also the editor of the Abilene paper remembered that the family

Dwight Eisenhower was made a four-star general in February 1943.

eventually became aware of Mamie's drinking and decided to intervene. "One close family member talked seriously to her," he recalled. . . . "She stopped at once."

When Ike was made a four-star general, Mamie found the other wives were jealous and that she had to be careful what she said around them. They, in turn, seemed to delight in relaying "news," which was usually scandal and gossip that could only hurt Mamie. Hurting the commander's wife, they believed, was one way of expressing their frustration that their own husbands weren't in charge.

Mamie resolved not to let the idle gossip get her down. For Ike's sake, she opened up to the press. She was photographed showing off her family scrapbooks, which included glowing stories of Ike. The press never knew there was any strain between her and her husband. They always found Mamie vivacious and "witty" as one reporter noted, ready to make sandwiches or iced tea. She once even noted jokingly that there were a few articles that *didn't* make it into her scrapbook, meaning those relating to Kay Summersby.

By early 1944, Ike was indeed "keeping busy," as he wrote to Mamie, with the planning of the D-Day invasion, which was to be the largest sea-to-land invasion in history. Of course,

The Eisenhowers' son John with his mother on the grounds of the Wardman Towers complex

he couldn't say anything about this directly. What she did know made her all the more keenly aware of the burden of Ike's responsibilities. She regretted that she'd made him worry about her own cares.

On June 6, 1944—D-Day, when the Allied forces landed in Normandy, France—Mamie was at West Point for John's graduation. At 7:00 A.M., the phone rang in her hotel room. "What do you think about the invasion?" a reporter asked. Mamie groggily remembered how she was supposed to answer: "No comment!" When she came down for breakfast, both she and John were hounded by nearly forty

General Eisenhower addressing paratroopers of the 101st Airborne Division in Newberry, England, shortly before the Normandy invasion on June 6, 1944

D-Day: "The Great Crusade"

★ ★

Early in World War II, the German army overran and occupied France and the smaller nations of Western Europe. To drive the Germans out, Allied leaders made a bold plan to attack the occupied lands with the largest sea-to-land, or amphibious, invasion in history. The United States and Britain secretly assembled 2.9 million men and tons of equipment, studied German defenses along the French coast, and waited for just the right moment to launch the huge assault. Finally, General Dwight Eisenhower—supreme commander of the Allied Expeditionary Forces— gave the go-ahead. The massive effort—called Operation Overlord— commenced. "You are about to embark on the Great Crusade," he advised his men. "The eyes of the world are upon you." In the predawn hours of D-Day, June 6, 1944, 4,000 landing craft, 600 warships, and 11,000 planes transported 175,000 soldiers and paratroopers across the stormy channel between England and France. The landing surprised the Germans, who expected an invasion farther up the coast. Nonetheless, as Allied troops swarmed the beaches, thousands of young men fell to enemy fire in the first few hours. The rest of the force pushed on into France, followed by wave after wave of reinforcements. By August 28, the Allies marched into Paris. Though the D-Day invasion led to the defeat of Germany, Eisenhower recognized its high risks, drafting a memo to be issued in the event of its failure. "If any blame or fault attaches to the attempt it is mine alone," he concluded.

Dwight Eisenhower was made a five-star general in December 1944.

Eisenhower and England's prime minister Winston Churchill met in France in September 1944.

reporters. Later that day, when John walked to the commencement podium to receive his diploma, loud applause greeted the name "Eisenhower."

At the end of 1944, Ike made a secret visit to Washington to confer with President Roosevelt, see Mamie, and take a needed break from his burdensome responsibilities. He'd been living in London for two and a half years, and while they were thrilled to be together again, both Ike and Mamie could admit that the war had been a strain on their marriage. He sneaked in and out of the apartment at Wardman Towers, prompting more than one rumor that *she* was having a love affair.

Despite all that tore them apart during the war, they used the few days together to talk about all they shared. To many friends and family members, they seemed to deepen their connection. Just before he went back to Europe, Ike gave Mamie a diamond watch that he'd been saving for ever since the war began. Still, despite a sense of renewal in their relationship, Mamie admitted that "he belonged to the world and not to me anymore."

CHAPTER SIX

America's Hero

✳ ✳ ✳ ✳ ✳ ✳ ✳ ✳ ✳ ✳ ✳ ✳ ✳ ✳ ✳

In a slide show of Ike and Mamie in the years just after the war, one would see image after image of an open convertible making its slow way down a big-city parade route. In each shot, Ike beams as he stands and waves to exuberant onlookers. Ticker tape and confetti fall from the tall buildings that line the street. Mamie, holding a bouquet of roses, sits on the seat next to "my boyfriend," as she still called the war hero.

Mamie was thrilled that Ike was getting the recognition he so clearly deserved. When someone told her, during that same time, that a popular magazine had polled its readers and named Ike the greatest living

✳ ✳ ✳ ✳ ✳ ✳ ✳ ✳ ✳ ✳ ✳ ✳ ✳ ✳ ✳

In the years just after the war, America's hero Dwight Eisenhower and his wife Mamie made their way down many big-city parade routes in an open convertible—Ike always standing and waving to the crowds.

American, Mamie said, "They didn't have to go to all that trouble. I could have told them."

When the parades, banquets, and ceremonies began to wind down, Dwight and Mamie Eisenhower could finally think about what would come next in their lives. After retiring from active military service in 1948 as the only five-star general in history, Ike accepted the post of president of Columbia University in New York City. The demands of college life didn't suit Ike, however. When he was asked, he was happy to resume military duties as the supreme commander of the North Atlantic Treaty Organization (NATO) forces in Europe. NATO was a military alliance that included the United States, Canada, and several Western European nations. As the decade of the 1950s began, Ike and Mamie were settling into yet another temporary home, this time in France.

In the United States in early 1952, the name "Eisenhower" was men-

John, Mamie, and Ike in their hotel in Scotland during a 1946 trip

John (left) and his father seeing the sights in Scotland in 1946

Mamie (front left, in an aisle seat) watches as her husband is about to be installed as president of New York City's Columbia University.

The North Atlantic Treaty Organization

✶ ✶

Even as the danger from Germany ended with World War II, another threat to world peace was growing. Europe lay in disarray after the war, its governments weakened, its cities destroyed, and its economy in ruins. Who would control post-war Europe? In the east, the communist Soviet Union, which had suffered greatly during the war, gobbled up the smaller nations on its borders and established communist governments there. These came to be known as Soviet "satellites." In Western Europe, the United States was determined to make sure that the people chose their own forms of government. An imaginary "iron curtain" separated east from west, dividing Europe into communist states and free states. Each felt threatened by the other, and the world plunged into a standoff called the Cold War. To discourage further Soviet aggression, twelve Western nations signed the North Atlantic Treaty on April 4, 1949. In it they agreed that "an armed attack against one or more of them . . . shall be considered an attack against them all." The new NATO alliance named General Dwight Eisenhower as the first Supreme Allied Commander Europe (SACEUR) in December 1950.

tioned often as a possible successor to Harry Truman, who had been president since Franklin Roosevelt's death in 1945. Both the Republicans and Democrats wanted Ike to lead their parties, but Ike, never a political man, decided he was a Republican since that's what everyone in Abilene, Kansas, had been.

When Dwight D. Eisenhower announced his intention to seek the Re-publican party's nomination for president in 1952, no one doubted that this national hero was the candidate to beat. For Mamie, Ike's entry into the political arena offered her an opportunity to make a real contribution. Finally, her naturally bubbly, extroverted personality could be front and center.

When the results of the 1952 election were in, no one was surprised that

Mamie poses in the salon of the Eisenhowers' new home in France when Ike was supreme commander of the North Atlantic Treaty Organization (NATO) in 1951–52.

President Harry S. Truman shaking hands with General Eisenhower, who was to be the next president of the United States

General Eisenhower had become president. To many, he seemed perfect for the prosperous, relaxed beginning of the 1950s, and his election had seemed somehow inevitable. Most Americans wanted to forget the long, dreary war years and focus on the lighter side of life. It was an era of poodle skirts, hula hoops, saddle shoes, and barbecue grills. Mamie,

Ike, Mamie, and Senator Henry Cabot Lodge Jr. (Ike's campaign manager) in Chicago during the Republican party convention in August 1952 when Eisenhower became the Republican candidate for president

President-elect Dwight D. Eisenhower and his wife, Mamie, show off newspaper headlines announcing his win.

The 1950s was an era of poodle skirts, hula hoops (above), saddle shoes, and penny loafers.

ever had was "Ike." She adored showing off her son John, his wife Barbara, and their children. She wasn't interested in politics or social causes—even though she did share strong opinions with close family and

President Eisenhower cooking ribs on a barbecue grill, another activity that began in the 1950s

who made no excuses for her love of frivolity, was glad the country was enjoying these new fads. She also thought the new "rock 'n' roll" music that was causing such a stir was just right for the young.

Mamie seemed the very picture of femininity and was a model that many middle-class American women wanted to emulate. Not only did she love the color pink and "girl-talk," but she bragged that the only career she'd

Mamie's daughter-in-law Barbara taking a Christmas 1952 picture of Mamie's mother, Elivera Doud, Mamie, and the three Eisenhower grandchildren

friends—but did love holding parties and receptions. She willingly invited women's clubs to the White House and often stood for hours shaking hands and chatting with each person in line.

Mamie adored being First Lady. She'd always loved being the center of attention, and now she was clearly that. She loved to ride around Washington in a limousine and wave to anyone who recognized her. In

First Lady Mamie Eisenhower thoroughly enjoyed being the center of attention and often waved from her limousine to anyone who recognized her.

parades, she rode in a car behind the president's, and when people asked Ike, "Where's Mamie?" she rolled her window down and shouted, "Here I am!" with clear delight.

Underneath her smiling girlishness, however, she was a strong-minded manager. From her "Mamie pink" bedroom, she gave orders that the staff learned to obey without hesitation. She was cool, efficient, and a close observer of everything around her. "Mrs. Eisenhower knows every single thing that goes on in this house. . . ." remarked one White House butler.

To suburban housewives, however, she was simply "one of them." She boasted about buying clothes off the

First Lady Mamie Eisenhower christening the first atom-powered submarine on January 1954

The Eisenhowers hosted a state dinner for the Shah and Princess Soraya of Iran in December 1954

First Lady Mamie Eisenhower and actress Mary Pickford kicked off a White House Defense Bond campaign in 1953.

Mamie at a USO fund-raiser in 1952

Surviving Suburbia

✶ ✶

In the early 1950s, America took a deep breath. Finally, life could return to normal. However, after ten years of the Great Depression of the 1930s and a decade of war and recovery in the 1940s, no one was sure what "normal" meant. Women who had filled in at jobs on the homefront while men went to war scrambled back to family life. Their husbands, on the other hand, hurried off to work in corporate America. Couples married and had children in record numbers, becoming the parents of the huge baby-boom generation.

In the midst of this, a new lifestyle was taking shape. Builder William Levitt, fascinated by uniform military housing, created on Long Island the first modern suburb. Levittown included 17,400 affordable homes, each a copy of the next, arranged in tidy rows over 4,000 acres (1,619 hectares). Similar communities sprang up around the country, making the American dream of home ownership available to a growing middle class. Backyard barbecues, PTA meetings, lawn-mowing, and cocktail parties set the rhythm of daily life.

For women, the suburbs were a mixed blessing. Quiet, safe places to raise children, these communities were also isolated. Located away from the cities, few of them had public transportation systems. Many suburban housewives found themselves hemmed in by their shiny modern kitchens and convenient appliances. The trend discouraged women from seeking fulfillment outside the home. Even seeking a higher education was often viewed as a way to meet a husband.

Nonetheless, so firmly did the suburban lifestyle take root that even the First Lady of the 1950s, Mamie Eisenhower, was proud to consider herself a suburban housewife.

sale racks, using coupons for groceries, and spending her afternoons watching television soap operas. She took special care with holidays, putting witches, goblins, and orange lights around on Halloween and pink bun-

Mamie and Ike outside the White House on their thirty-eighth wedding anniversary, July 1, 1954

nies on every mantelpiece at Easter. She greeted guests wearing green on St. Patrick's Day and had green carnations hung from the chandeliers. She wore charm bracelets and spike heels and liked to say, "Ike runs the country, I turn the pork chops."

Despite her enthusiasm for life in the White House, Mamie knew the pressures of the presidency were burdensome for Ike. Mamie insisted that he leave his work behind when he returned to their White House living quarters. "When Ike came home, he came home," she once said. "I never went to his headquarters when he was an army officer. I only went to his White House office four times—and I was invited each time." Mamie and Ike often ate their dinner on trays in front of the television, and they laughed uproariously at popular shows such as *I Love Lucy* and *Your Show of Shows*.

Even before Ike became president, he and Mamie had searched for a house to buy—one that was to be both their first and their last true home. In 1951, they bought a large dairy farm in Gettysburg, Pennsylvania. For the next few years, Mamie oversaw the work of turning the two-story white brick farmhouse into "Mamie's dream house." In 1955, the renovations were complete, and the Eisenhowers began spending weekends and holidays there, often with invited guests. Among those who signed Mamie's guest book were Charles de Gaulle, president of France, and Nikita Khrushchev, premier of the Soviet Union.

At Home on the Battlefield

✮ ✮

After a lifetime of temporary quarters, the Eisenhowers craved a permanent home. In 1950, they found one amid the rolling hills of southern Pennsylvania close to the Maryland border. There they purchased for $24,000 a century-old dairy farm situated on 189 acres (76 ha). The couple had come to know and love the rural countryside when Eisenhower commanded nearby Camp Colt during World War I. Perhaps what moved them most, however, was the farm's location overlooking the historic Gettysburg battlefield. Here, in one of the most important battles of the Civil War, Northern troops crushed Robert E. Lee's Confederate army, turning the tide of war in favor of the North. More than 50,000 soldiers died at Gettysburg during that three-day battle in 1863, and the grounds have been preserved since then as a national cemetery and memorial park. The farmhouse purchased by the Eisenhowers survived the battle, but by 1950 was too run-down to live in. Ike and Mamie built a new brick house around it and enjoyed the home as a retreat throughout his presidency. After they retired there in 1961, Eisenhower raised Black Angus show cattle on the ample grounds. Today, the farm is a national historic, site preserved as the Eisenhowers left it, still overlooking the slumbering battlefield at Gettysburg.

Yet that same year, 1955, Ike began to learn the price of being everyone's hero. On a vacation trip to Denver, he was rushed to the hospital after complaining of indigestion and chest pains. Within a few hours, a shocked nation learned that President Eisenhower had suffered a heart attack. He spent the next six weeks in a Denver hospital. Mamie stood watch over the stricken leader, making sure unnecessary demands weren't made on him. When his recovery was complete, Ike had a brooch ("a military medal," he called it) made at Tiffany's and gave it to Mamie for her "devotion to the nation's commander in chief."

Mamie had long opposed the idea

Ike and Mamie bought this farmhouse in Gettysburg, Pennsylvania, in 1951.

This Chicago Daily News *headline let the city know of the president's 1955 heart attack.*

United States president Dwight D. Eisenhower with Soviet premier Nikita Khrushchev

Mamie showing off a "Stick With Ike" sticker at the 1956 Republican National Convention

President Eisenhower and First Lady Mamie Eisenhower on the White House grounds, Easter 1956

of Ike seeking a second term in office. But during his recuperation, she saw how difficult it was for him to be idle. She began to worry that retirement might harm him even more. Privately, she longed to leave the public eye, but when Ike asked her about a second term, she told him to "follow his own wishes." Ike decided to run again and was elected easily in 1956.

When the Eisenhowers left the White House in 1960, Ike's last term seemed tinged by disappointment and sadness. He was dismayed at the rapid escalation of the Cold War between the United States and the Soviet Union. He had warned a skeptical nation that America should not invest all its energy in developing new weapons and bombs. He believed that because of his own military background, his words would carry weight. But his warnings were largely ignored. Racial conflict in the South also seemed beyond his ability to fully understand or control. As violence

First Lady Mamie Eisenhower with a group of fifty-seven women guests at a luncheon honoring women members of the United Nations

against black people became commonplace throughout the South, the president had been unable to lessen the fierce hatred that fueled it.

Both Ike and Mamie supported the candidacy of Vice President Richard Nixon and were disappointed when he lost the presidential election of 1960 to John F. Kennedy. Mamie believed that Nixon's defeat was a personal affront to Ike. She disliked the boyish president-elect and complained that his wife, Jackie, clearly spent too much money on clothes. Days before the inauguration, Mamie complained loudly when her favorite soap opera was

Democratic presidential candidate John F. Kennedy and his wife Jackie campaigning in 1960

Former president Dwight Eisenhower golfing in Scotland in 1962

interrupted for a special about Mrs. Kennedy and the upcoming inaugural festivities. Nor did Mamie appreciate constant mention of the fact that Mrs. Kennedy was the first First Lady born in the twentieth century—and that Mamie Eisenhower was the last born during the nineteenth.

On Inauguration Day 1961, Ike and Mamie got into their five-year-old Chrysler and were driven away from the snow-covered Executive Mansion to their farm in Gettysburg. During the next few years, they lived out the

Ike painting on the back porch of the Eisenhower home in Gettysburg, Pennsylvania

This charming 1966 photograph of the Eisenhowers was taken at their retirement home in Gettysburg, Pennsylvania.

A group photo of Mamie (front row, second from left) and Dwight Eisenhower (back row, second from right) with their family

retirement they'd long dreamed of, surrounded by grandchildren and old family friends. Ike played golf, fished, painted, and even cooked. Yet leisure time did not improve his health, which declined steadily throughout the 1960s.

By 1968, Ike was spending most of his time in and out of the hospital. "Ike knew he was dying," Mamie said. He died at Walter Reed Army Medical Center in Washington, D.C., on March 8, 1969, surrounded by his family and holding Mamie's hand.

Mamie Eisenhower and her son John just after the last rites for Dwight Eisenhower in Abilene, Kansas

This picture of Mamie, next to a picture of her with Ike, was taken on her seventy-third birthday in 1969.

Mamie lived ten years longer, spending most of her time at the Gettysburg farm, where she said, "I miss him every day." She died on November 1, 1979, and was buried beside Ike and their first-born son, Icky, in Abilene, Kansas. "She had the guts to be her classic self," stated a published obituary. "She was *Mamie*."

Mamie posed for this picture next to a portrait of her husband, former president Dwight D. Eisenhower, in May 1974.

Profile of America, 1979: An Anxious Nation

✩ ✩

Mamie Eisenhower died in the last, troubled year of the 1970s. After several years battling inflation, an energy crisis, and rampant unemployment, Americans felt wrung out. Prices rose and jobs dwindled; foreign competition in the automobile and other industries taxed American corporations and workers further. Even President Jimmy Carter was unable to reverse the depressing economic trends.

In March, an accident at the Three Mile Island nuclear power plant in Pennsylvania shook Americans from coast to coast. Thousands fled the area and an anxious nation watched and waited to see how the crisis would end. Though the failure was contained over the course of twelve days and only a small amount of radioactivity escaped, the potential for nuclear meltdown or explosion had come frighteningly close to reality. While it took ten years to decontaminate the site, the public image of nuclear power may never recover. In July, more fallout from modern technology threatened as Skylab began to descend uncontrolled from its six-year earth orbit. Thankfully, the space station crashed harmlessly in pieces into the Indian Ocean.

In the fall, another catastrophe tested the nerves of the nation. On November 4, militant Iranians overran the American Embassy in their nation's revolution-torn capital. They held fifty-two American citizens for 444 days in what came to be called the "hostage crisis." President Carter proved powerless in negotiating their return. An anxious nation decorated with yellow ribbons waited until Ronald Reagan's inauguration in 1981 for their release. The crisis triggered an oil shortage that forced drivers to line up at the pumps for their share of gasoline.

Anxiety crept into American leisure time as well. The most popular movies of 1979 included *Star Trek, Apocalypse Now, Alien,* and *The China Syndrome* (the last about a nuclear disaster). But the movie of the year turned out to be *Kramer vs. Kramer,* a realistic and moving tale about modern divorce. With divorce rates up 69 percent over the last decade, the movie touched the growing number of single parents. Meanwhile, a song called "We Are Family" by Sister Sledge topped the charts.

In 1979, Americans were reading Tom Wolfe's *The Right Stuff* and William Styron's *Sophie's Choice.* They watched as *Voyager 1* and *Voyager 2* sped past Jupiter and photographed its moons. They listened to brand-new Sony Walkman radios on their morning jogs and endlessly played a board game called Trivial Pursuit, which tested one's knowledge of insignificant facts. On the basketball court, two young stars collided when Indiana State met Michigan State in the NCAA championship. Larry Bird outscored Earvin "Magic" Johnson to give ISU the title.

The Presidents and Their First Ladies

YEARS IN OFFICE			
President	*Birth–Death*	*First Lady*	*Birth–Death*
1789–1797			
George Washington	1732–1799	Martha Dandridge Custis Washington	1731–1802
1797–1801			
John Adams	1735–1826	Abigail Smith Adams	1744–1818
1801–1809			
Thomas Jefferson†	1743–1826		
1809–1817			
James Madison	1751–1836	Dolley Payne Todd Madison	1768–1849
1817–1825			
James Monroe	1758–1831	Elizabeth Kortright Monroe	1768–1830
1825–1829			
John Quincy Adams	1767–1848	Louisa Catherine Johnson Adams	1775–1852
1829–1837			
Andrew Jackson†	1767–1845		
1837–1841			
Martin Van Buren†	1782–1862		
1841			
William Henry Harrison‡	1773–1841		
1841–1845			
John Tyler	1790–1862	Letitia Christian Tyler (1841–1842)	1790–1842
		Julia Gardiner Tyler (1844–1845)	1820–1889
1845–1849			
James K. Polk	1795–1849	Sarah Childress Polk	1803–1891
1849–1850			
Zachary Taylor	1784–1850	Margaret Mackall Smith Taylor	1788–1852
1850–1853			
Millard Fillmore	1800–1874	Abigail Powers Fillmore	1798–1853
1853–1857			
Franklin Pierce	1804–1869	Jane Means Appleton Pierce	1806–1863
1857–1861			
James Buchanan*	1791–1868		
1861–1865			
Abraham Lincoln	1809–1865	Mary Todd Lincoln	1818–1882
1865–1869			
Andrew Johnson	1808–1875	Eliza McCardle Johnson	1810–1876
1869–1877			
Ulysses S. Grant	1822–1885	Julia Dent Grant	1826–1902
1877–1881			
Rutherford B. Hayes	1822–1893	Lucy Ware Webb Hayes	1831–1889
1881			
James A. Garfield	1831–1881	Lucretia Rudolph Garfield	1832–1918
1881–1885			
Chester A. Arthur†	1829–1886		

† wife died before he took office ‡ wife too ill to accompany him to Washington * never married

1885–1889			
Grover Cleveland	1837–1908	Frances Folsom Cleveland	1864–1947
1889–1893			
Benjamin Harrison	1833–1901	Caroline Lavinia Scott Harrison	1832–1892
1893–1897			
Grover Cleveland	1837–1908	Frances Folsom Cleveland	1864–1947
1897–1901			
William McKinley	1843–1901	Ida Saxton McKinley	1847–1907
1901–1909			
Theodore Roosevelt	1858–1919	Edith Kermit Carow Roosevelt	1861–1948
1909–1913			
William Howard Taft	1857–1930	Helen Herron Taft	1861–1943
1913–1921			
Woodrow Wilson	1856–1924	Ellen Louise Axson Wilson (1913–1914)	1860–1914
		Edith Bolling Galt Wilson (1915–1921)	1872–1961
1921–1923			
Warren G. Harding	1865–1923	Florence Kling Harding	1860–1924
1923–1929			
Calvin Coolidge	1872–1933	Grace Anna Goodhue Coolidge	1879–1957
1929–1933			
Herbert Hoover	1874–1964	Lou Henry Hoover	1874–1944
1933–1945			
Franklin D. Roosevelt	1882–1945	Anna Eleanor Roosevelt	1884–1962
1945–1953			
Harry S. Truman	1884–1972	Bess Wallace Truman	1885–1982
1953–1961			
Dwight D. Eisenhower	1890–1969	Mamie Geneva Doud Eisenhower	1896–1979
1961–1963			
John F. Kennedy	1917–1963	Jacqueline Bouvier Kennedy	1929–1994
1963–1969			
Lyndon B. Johnson	1908–1973	Claudia Taylor (Lady Bird) Johnson	1912–
1969–1974			
Richard Nixon	1913–1994	Patricia Ryan Nixon	1912–1993
1974–1977			
Gerald Ford	1913–	Elizabeth Bloomer Ford	1918–
1977–1981			
James Carter	1924–	Rosalynn Smith Carter	1927–
1981–1989			
Ronald Reagan	1911–	Nancy Davis Reagan	1923–
1989–1993			
George Bush	1924–	Barbara Pierce Bush	1925–
1993–			
William Jefferson Clinton	1946–	Hillary Rodham Clinton	1947–

Mamie Doud Eisenhower Timeline

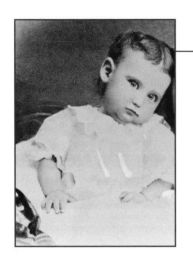

1896	★	First Ford automobile is built in Detroit
		William McKinley is elected president
		Mamie Doud is born on November 14
1898	★	Spanish-American War is fought, resulting in the United States annexing Puerto Rico, Guam, and the Philippines
1900	★	William McKinley is reelected president
1901	★	President McKinley is assassinated
		Theodore Roosevelt becomes president
1903	★	Wright brothers fly their airplane for the first time
1904	★	Theodore Roosevelt is elected president
1908	★	William Howard Taft is elected president
1909	★	National Association for the Advancement of Colored People (NAACP) is founded
1912	★	*Titanic* sinks in the North Atlantic
		Woodrow Wilson is elected president
1913	★	Henry Ford sets up his first assembly line
1914	★	Panama Canal is completed
		World War I begins
1915	★	*Lusitania* is sunk by a German submarine
1916	★	Mamie Doud marries Dwight D. Eisenhower
		Woodrow Wilson is reelected president
		National Park Service is established
1917	★	Doud Dwight (Icky) Eisenhower is born
		United States enters World War I
1918	★	United States and its allies win World War I

1920	★	Warren G. Harding is elected president
1921	★	Doud Dwight (Icky) Eisenhower dies
1922	★	First woman is appointed to the U.S. Senate
1923	★	John Sheldon Doud Eisenhower is born President Harding dies Calvin Coolidge becomes president
1924	★	Calvin Coolidge is elected president
1927	★	Charles Lindbergh flies solo across the Atlantic Ocean
1928	★	Herbert Hoover is elected president
1929	★	Stock market crashes, which starts the Great Depression
1932	★	Amelia Earhart becomes the first woman to fly solo across the Atlantic Ocean Franklin D. Roosevelt is elected president
1933	★	President Roosevelt begins the New Deal
1935	★	Congress passes the Social Security Act
1936	★	Franklin D. Roosevelt is reelected president
1937	★	Golden Gate Bridge is dedicated in San Francisco
1939	★	World War II begins
1940	★	Franklin D. Roosevelt is reelected president
1941	★	Japanese bomb Pearl Harbor United States enters World War II
1942	★	Dwight D. Eisenhower is appointed commanding general, European Theater of Operations; and commander in chief of Allied forces in North Africa
1943	★	Dwight D. Eisenhower is appointed supreme commander, Allied Expeditionary Forces
1944	★	Allies liberate Rome Dwight D. Eisenhower leads Allies in D-Day invasion of Europe Franklin D. Roosevelt is reelected president

1945	☆	President Roosevelt dies
		Harry S. Truman becomes president
		General Eisenhower accepts surrender of German army; World War II ends in Europe
		United States drops atomic bombs on Japan
		Japan surrenders, ending World War II
1947	☆	Jackie Robinson becomes the first African American to play major-league baseball
1948	☆	Marshall Plan extends aid to war-torn Europe
		Harry S. Truman is elected president
1949	☆	North Atlantic Treaty Organization (NATO) is formed
		United Nations Headquarters is dedicated in New York City
1950	☆	President Truman sends U.S. forces to fight in Korean War
1952	☆	Dwight D. Eisenhower is elected president
1953	☆	Korean War ends
1954	☆	Supreme Court declares segregated schools to be unconstitutional
1956	☆	Dwight D. Eisenhower is reelected president
1957	☆	Eisenhower Doctrine is formulated
		U.S. troops help desegregate Central High School in Little Rock, Arkansas
1958	☆	Recession cripples U.S. economy
1959	☆	Nikita Khrushchev visits the United States
1960	☆	John F. Kennedy is elected president
1961	☆	Eisenhowers retire to their farm in Gettysburg, Pennsylvania
		First Americans fly in space
		United States sends aid and advisors to South Vietnam
1963	☆	John F. Kennedy is assassinated
		Lyndon B. Johnson becomes president

1964	☆	Civil Rights Act is signed
		Lyndon B. Johnson is elected president
1965	☆	Malcolm X is assassinated
		United States sends troops to Vietnam
		Riots break out in the Watts neighborhood of Los Angeles
1966	☆	Medicare Act is signed
		United States has 400,000 troops in Vietnam
1967	☆	Antiwar protest is held at the Pentagon
1968	☆	Civil Rights Act is signed
		Martin Luther King Jr. and Robert F. Kennedy are assassinated
		Richard M. Nixon is elected president
1969	☆	Dwight D. Eisenhower dies
		President Nixon begins withdrawing U.S. soldiers from Vietnam
1970	☆	Antiwar protests rock college campuses
1972	☆	Last U.S. ground troops are withdrawn from Vietnam
		Burglary at the Watergate Complex is reported
		Richard Nixon is reelected president
1973	☆	Vice President Spiro Agnew resigns
		Gerald R. Ford becomes vice president
1974	☆	Richard M. Nixon resigns from office
		Gerald R. Ford becomes president
1975	☆	South Vietnam falls to the Communists
1976	☆	United States celebrates its bicentennial
		Jimmy Carter is elected president
1977	☆	President Carter pardons Vietnam War draft evaders
1978	☆	People's Republic of China and the United States begin full diplomatic ties
1979	☆	Mamie Doud Eisenhower dies on November 1

Fast Facts about
Mamie Doud Eisenhower

Born: November 14, 1896, in Boone, Iowa

Died: November 1, 1979, in Washington, D.C.

Burial Site: Abilene, Kansas

Parents: John Sheldon Doud and Elivera Carlson Doud

Education: Corona Street School; East Denver High School; Mulholland School (San Antonio); Miss Wolcott's finishing school (Denver)

Marriage: To Dwight D. Eisenhower from July 1, 1916, until his death on March 28, 1969

Children: Doud Dwight (Icky) Eisenhower (1917–1921) and John Sheldon Doud Eisenhower (1923–present)

Places She Lived: Boone, Iowa (1896–1897); Cedar Rapids, Iowa (1897–1904); Colorado Springs, Colorado (1904–1906); Denver, Colorado (1906–1916); San Antonio, Texas (1916–1917, 1941–1942, and winters of 1910–1915); Leavenworth, Kansas (1917–1918, 1925–1926); Gettysburg, Pennsylvania (1918–1919, 1955–1979); Fort Meade, Maryland (1919–1922); Panama Canal Zone (1922–1924); Washington, D.C. (1927–1928, 1930–1935, 1942–1945, 1953–1961); France (1928–1929, 1951–1952); Manila, Philippines (1936–1940); Tacoma, Washington (1940–1941); Arlington, Virginia (1942; 1945–1948); New York City (1948–1950, 1952)

Major Achievements:

* Brought formality to official White House functions but made the family's living quarters more functional and comfortable.
* Insisted on decorum by the White House staff but remembered staff members' birthdays with a card and a cake baked in the White House kitchen.
* Arranged the baptism of granddaughter Mary Jean Eisenhower in the Blue Room of the White House.
* Held many receptions and often shook hands with 600 to 700 people a day.
* Entertained more than seventy official foreign visitors.
* Promoted the work of the American Heart Association and served as its honorary national chairperson (1957–1961).

Fast Facts about
Dwight D. Eisenhower's Presidency

Terms of Office: Elected president of the United States in 1952 and reelected in 1956; served as the thirty-fourth president from 1953 to 1961

Vice President: Richard M. Nixon (1953–1961)

Major Policy Decisions and Legislation:

 * Signed the act that created the Department of Health, Education, and Welfare (April 1, 1953) and appointed Oveta Culp Hobby as its first secretary (April 11, 1953), the second woman appointed to a cabinet post.
 * Signed the St. Lawrence Seaway Act (May 13, 1954).
 * Signed the act that began construction of the interstate highway system (1956).
 * Signed Civil Rights Acts (1957 and 1960).
 * Placed the Arkansas National Guard under presidential command and ordered federal troops to Little Rock, Arkansas, to enforce desegregation at Central High School (September 1957).

Major Events:

 * Julius and Ethel Rosenberg were executed as spies (June 19, 1953).
 * *Nautilus*, the first nuclear submarine, was launched at Groton, Connecticut (January 21, 1954).
 * Earl Warren was confirmed as chief justice of the U.S. Supreme Court (1954). The following were confirmed as associate justices of the U.S. Supreme Court: John Marshall Harlan (1955), William Joseph Brennan (1957), Charles Evan Whittaker (1957), and Potter Stewart (1959). President Eisenhower appointed all five of these justices.
 * The Supreme Court declared racial segregation in U.S. public schools unconstitutional in the case *Brown v. Board of Education of Topeka* (May 17, 1954).
 * Alaska and Hawaii became the 49th and 50th states (1959).

103

Where to Visit

The Capitol Building
Constitution Avenue
Washington, D.C. 20510
(202) 225-3121

Dwight D. Eisenhower Library &
Museum
400 Southeast Fourth Street
Abilene, Kansas 67410
Phone: (785) 263-4751
Toll Free: 1-877-Ring Ike
e-mail: Library@eisenhower.nara.gov

Eisenhower National Historic Site
97 Taneytown Road
Gettysburg, Pennsylvania 17325
Phone: (717) 338-9114
Fax: (717) 338-0821
e-mail: eise_site_manager@nps.gov

Mamie Doud Eisenhower Birthplace
709 Carroll Street
Boone, Iowa 50036
Phone: (515) 432-1896

Museum of American History of the
Smithsonian Institution
"First Ladies: Political and Public Image"
14th St. and Constitution Avenue NW
Washington, D.C.
(202) 357-2008

National Archives
Constitution Avenue
Washington, D.C. 20408
(202) 501-5000

The National First Ladies Library
The Saxton McKinley House
331 South Market Avenue
Canton, Ohio 44702

White House
1600 Pennsylvania Avenue
Washington, D.C. 20500
Visitor's Office: (202) 456-7041

White House Historical Association
740 Jackson Place NW
Washington, D.C. 20503
(202) 737-8292

Online Sites of Interest

The First Ladies of the United States of America
http://www2.whitehouse.gov/WH/glimpse/firstladies/html/firstladies.html
Includes a portrait and biographical sketch of each First Lady plus links to other White House sites

Dwight David Eisenhower Library & Museum
http://www.eisenhower.utexas.edu/contents/htm
This museum in Abilene, Kansas, makes available the memorabilia of President and Mrs. Dwight Eisenhower. Includes links to general information, online photos, museum programs, and more.

Eisenhower National Historic Site
http://www.nps.gov/eise/
The farm in Gettysburg, Pennsylvania, was a meeting place for world leaders during Eisenhower's presidency and a retirement home from 1961 to 1969.

Internet Public Library, Presidents of the United States (IPL POTUS)
http://www.ipl.org/ref/POTUS/ddeisenhower.html
An excellent site with much information on Eisenhower and many links

Mamie Doud Eisenhower Birthplace
http://www.BooneIowa.com/mamie/
This Boone, Iowa, birthplace site includes information on location, tours, fees; a biography of Mamie Geneva Doud Eisenhower; a discussion of the restoration of her birthplace; and highlights of the house itself.

The National First Ladies Library
http://www.firstladies.org
The first virtual library devoted to the lives and legacies of America's First Ladies, including much information about First Ladies and a tour of the restored Saxton McKinley House in Canton, Ohio, which houses the library.

The White House
http://www.whitehouse.gov/WH/glimpse/top.html
Information and biographies of current and past presidents, White House history and tours, current events, and more.

The White House for Kids
http://www.whitehouse.gov/WH/kids/html/kidshome.html
Information about White House kids, First Pets, historic moments, issues of a White House newsletter, and more.

For Further Reading

Black, Wallace B. *D-Day*. New York: Crestwood House, 1992.

David, Lester and Irene David. *Ike and Mamie: The Story of the General and His Lady*. New York: G. P. Putnam's Sons, 1981.

Dolan, Edward F. *America in World War I*. Brookfield, Conn.: Millbrook Press, 1996.

Gormley, Beatrice. *First Ladies*. New York: Scholastic, Inc., 1997.

Gould, Lewis L. (ed.). *American First Ladies: Their Lives and Their Legacy*. New York: Garland Publishing, 1996.

Hargrove, Jim. *Dwight D. Eisenhower: Thirty-Fourth President of the United States*. Encyclopedia of Presidents. Chicago: Childrens Press, 1987.

Jacobs, William Jay. *Dwight David Eisenhower: Soldier and Statesman*. New York: Franklin Watts, 1995.

Jacobson, Doranne. *Presidents and First Ladies of the United States*. New York: Smithmark Publishers, Inc., 1995.

Klapthor, Margaret Brown. *The First Ladies*. Washington, D.C.: White House Historical Association, 1994.

Mayo, Edith P. (ed.). *The Smithsonian Book of the First Ladies: Their Lives, Times, and Issues*. New York: Henry Holt, 1996.

McGowen, Tom. *World War II*. New York: Franklin Watts, 1993.

Sandak, Cass. *The Eisenhowers*. New York: Crestwood House, 1993.

Stewart, Gail B. *World War I*. America's Wars series. San Diego: Lucent Books, 1991.

Index

Page numbers in **boldface type** indicate illustrations

Photo Identifications

Cover: Official White House portrait of Mamie Doud Eisenhower by Thomas E. Stephens
Page 8: Mamie Eisenhower wearing her inaugural gown
Page 18: Mamie Doud at the age of fourteen
Page 32: Lieutenant Dwight David Eisenhower and Mamie Geneva Doud at the time of their marriage on July 1, 1916
Page 44: An undated portrait of Mamie Doud Eisenhower
Page 60: A 1944 photograph of Mamie Doud Eisenhower
Page 72: Official White House portrait of Mamie Doud Eisenhower by Thomas E. Stephens

Photo Credits©

About the Author

Susan Sinnott began her publishing career as an editor for *Cricket*, a literary magazine for children. She later worked for the University of Wisconsin Press, where she managed and edited academic journals. Eventually, her own children pulled her away from scholarly publishing and helped her rediscover the joys of reading and writing books for young people. Ms. Sinnott's books include two previous Encyclopedia of First Ladies books, *Sara Childress Polk* and *Frances Folsom Cleveland* as well as *Extraordinary Hispanic Americans* and *Extraordinary Asian Pacific Americans* for Children's Press; and *Chinese Railroad Workers* and *Doing Our Part: American Women on the Home Front During World War II* for Franklin Watts.